13.45
3-05

Economy and Industry
IN ANCIENT EGYPT

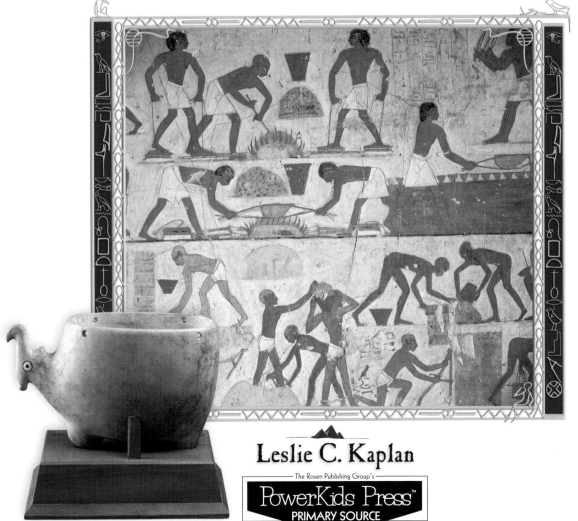

Leslie C. Kaplan

The Rosen Publishing Group's
PowerKids Press™
PRIMARY SOURCE

New York

To Kim and Danny

Published in 2004 by The Rosen Publishing Group, Inc.
29 East 21st Street, New York, NY 10010

First Edition

Editor: Rachel O'Connor
Book Design: Maria E. Melendez
Photo Researcher: Adriana Skura

Photo Credits: Cover and pp. 4, 15 © Erich Lessing/Art Resource, NY, cover (inset) and pp. 12, 20 (center) ©Scala/Art Resource, NY; pp. 4 (inset), 7 (bottom), 8 The Art Archive/Dagli Orti; pp. 7 (top), 16 (top right), 20 (top left) The Art Archive/Egyptian Museum Cairo/Dagli Orti; p. 7 (center) The Art Archive/Musee du Louvre Paris; p. 11 © Cameraphoto/Art Resource, NY; pp. 11 (inset), 19 ©Werner Forman/Art Resource, NY; p.12 (inset) The Art Archive/Egyptian Museum Turin/Dagli Orti; p. 16 (top left) © Giraudon/Art Resource, NY, (bottom) The Art Archive/Jacqueline Hyde; p. 20 (bottom) The Art Archive/Staatliche Sammlung Agyptischer Kunst Munich/Dagli Orti.

Kaplan, Leslie C.
Economy and industry in ancient Egypt / Leslie C. Kaplan.—1st ed.
     p. cm.—(Primary sources of ancient civilizations. Egypt)
Includes bibliographical references and index.
  ISBN 0-8239-6786-7 ((library binding)—ISBN 0-8239-8936-4 (pbk.)
1. Egypt—Economic conditions—332 B.C.-640 A.D. 2. Industries—Egypt—History. I. Title. II. Primary sources of ancient civilizations. Egypt.
  HC33.K36 2004
  330.932'01—dc21

                                                                    2003002331

Manufactured in the United States of America

J932

Contents

This fresco shows Egyptians fishing. The fishers would stand in papyrus canoes, ready to catch the fish with their harpoons.

This wall painting is taken from the tomb of Rekhmire, a nobleman from the Eighteenth Dynasty (1567-1320 B.C.). It shows craftsmen using various tools and raw materials to build a temple.

Ancient Egypt's economy was mostly centered around agriculture. Egypt's warm climate and the yearly flooding of the Nile River allowed for as many as three harvests per year. Also, the Nile and the surrounding land provided natural resources such as mud, papyrus, flax, gold, and stone. The ancient Egyptians were able to create important goods and services with these raw materials. As a result, many skilled craftsmen and merchants began to appear. Builders built homes from mud bricks and made tombs and temples with stone. Craftsmen made jewelry from gold, clothing from flax, and pottery from earth.

The fertile soil of Egypt produced most of the land's wealth. Corn, wheat, and barley were among the most widely cultivated crops. Vegetables grown in great quantities included cucumbers, onions, lettuces, beans, and peas. Popular fruits were figs, grapes, dates, pomegranates, and melons. Cattle and sheep were a source of meat and dairy products, and the Nile provided the Egyptians with plenty of fish. Successful farming in ancient Egypt meant that everyone had enough to eat and that other businesses were able to develop. Leftover crops provided the raw materials for many industries in ancient Egypt and helped to develop trade and export.

In this scene taken from an Eighteenth-Dynasty tomb, a royal subject is shown leading an ox. Oxen were important to Egyptian farmers. The oxen helped to cultivate the land and increase productivity.

This fresco shows Egyptians hard at work harvesting grain. Barley was the main grain grown. Egyptians used barley to make bread and beer. They traded any leftover grains.

In this sculpture from the tomb of Ti, an Egyptian official, farmworkers are making haystacks.

Goldsmiths weigh gold and present their work in this fresco taken from the tomb of sculptors Nebamon and Ipuky. Egyptians bartered their gold for goods such as silver, iron, and horses from southwest Asia. Much of Egypt's gold came from the hills east of the Nile River.

The Barter System

Money did not exist in ancient Egypt. Instead of making purchases, the Egyptians traded their goods and services. This is called bartering. Most of the trading between Egyptians simply involved swapping one object for another. Farmworkers received wheat and barley in payment for their work. They could exchange a bag of grain to get pottery from a craftsman or clothing from a weaver. Fishers might trade some of their catch from the Nile River in exchange for other goods. It was not until about 1580 B.C. that the Egyptians began to give certain values to gold, copper, and imported silver so that these metals could be used as money.

The Egyptians traded with lands outside of Egypt. They exported goods to lands bordering the Aegean, Mediterranean, and Red Seas, among others. Egypt's main exports included grain, vegetables, and gold. Gold, found in many parts of Egypt, was a valuable export since it was rare in regions outside of Egypt. Other important exports were linen made from the flax plant, paper made from papyrus, and pottery crafted from mud. Industries flourished in ancient Egypt as craftsmen developed businesses that provided goods for export. Egyptians traded their goods for items that were scarce in Egypt, such as wood, silver, iron, ivory, and spices.

In this map we can see how close Egypt is to the Mediterranean Sea. This closeness greatly helped Egypt's trading practices.

Drawn on the tomb of Nefer and Kahay, this wall painting shows ancient Egyptian farmers harvesting papyrus. This involved binding the papyrus in bunches, moving it, and peeling it.

This is what a rolled piece of papyrus paper looks like. The stone tool below was used to make paper from papyrus.

Popular Papyrus

The papyrus plant greatly helped the growth of ancient Egypt's economy. Papyrus grew along the Nile and provided the raw material for goods such as paper, boats, and baskets. Paper was the most important product made from papyrus. Historians believe that papyrus paper was first used around 2400 B.C. It was the only kind of paper until around the second century B.C., when a new paper, made from bamboo, was invented in China. Papyrus paper was one of Egypt's main exports to places such as Greece and Rome. Egyptian kings did not want other nations to know how to make paper from papyrus. That way the demand for paper would remain high.

Mud from the banks of the Nile was used in the building industry in ancient Egypt. Workers made bricks from the mud to build all types of houses. Brickmaking was considered a lowly job in Egypt, since it did not require special training. Craftsmen, such as potters, also used mud to make clay. With the clay, the potters made kitchenware such as cups, bowls, jars, and vases. Potters were considered manual laborers, since they made a product that was meant to be used in daily life. Egyptians from all social classes used the pottery in their homes. Pottery was also exported, since it was popular overseas.

This detail of a painting on the tomb wall of nobleman Rekhmire shows potters as they decorate a vase.

Egyptian vases were used to store water, wine, oil, or grain.

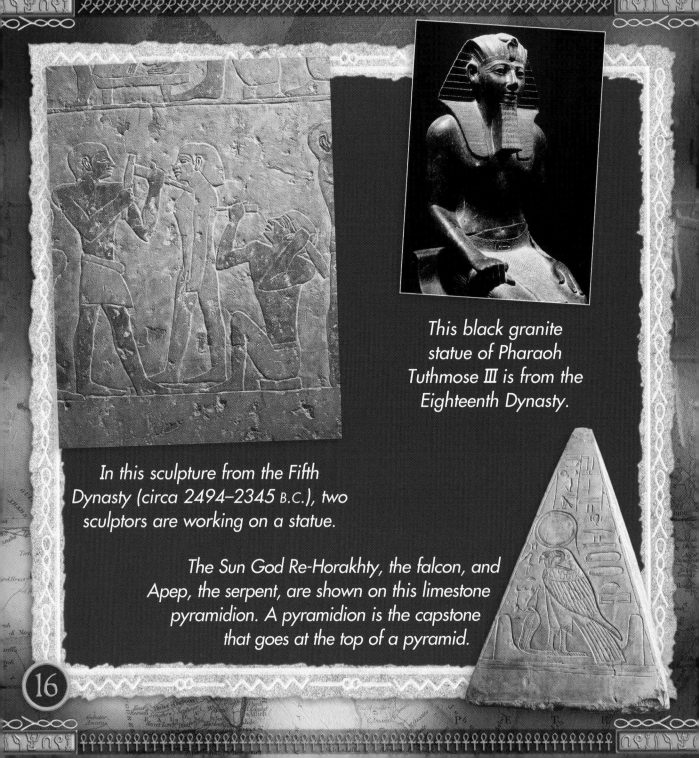

This black granite statue of Pharaoh Tuthmose III is from the Eighteenth Dynasty.

In this sculpture from the Fifth Dynasty (circa 2494–2345 B.C.), two sculptors are working on a statue.

The Sun God Re-Horakhty, the falcon, and Apep, the serpent, are shown on this limestone pyramidion. A pyramidion is the capstone that goes at the top of a pyramid.

Egypt's stonecutting industry was made possible by the large, plentiful supplies of such stone as limestone and granite. Highly skilled stoneworkers built statues, tombs, temples, and pyramids for the royal family and upper classes. People from the lowest classes often could not afford stone tombs or statues. However, they bought stone vases, jugs, and pots from craftsmen who made such objects. Stoneware was not used much, if at all, in daily life. It was highly valued and was meant to furnish tombs. The royal family's need for a stonecutter's work made the stonecutting industry one of Egypt's most important businesses.

Making Cloth

The linen industry in Egypt developed because of the large amounts of the flax plant. Flax was an inexpensive raw material for making clothes. Many families grew their own flax and made linen at home. Egyptians were among the first of the ancient civilizations to develop a linen industry, making linen for trade at home and overseas. Egyptian women worked in the shops that were set up for weaving and spinning cloth. Egyptian weavers used metal knives and needles to make garments. Linen is a soft, light cloth. It was a good material to wear in Egypt's hot, desert climate. It was also a popular export item, supporting the growth of Egypt's economy.

This is a wooden model of a weaver's workshop from the Eleventh Dynasty (circa 2133–1991 B.C.). It shows two women using a tool for weaving cloth, called a loom. Other women spin thread or wind skeins, which are balls of thread, for weaving.

From the Twelfth Dynasty (1991–1786 B.C.), this gold and enamel snake was worn on the front of the crown of King Sesostris II.

The funeral collar shown here is from the tomb of Pharaoh Tutankhamen. These colored beads are most likely made from faience, or jewelry made from quartz.

This gold and enamel bracelet, featuring the goddess Isis as the central design, is from the pyramid of Queen Amanishakheto.

A Big Market for Jewelry

The rulers of Egypt had a love for jewelry that kept many craftsmen in jobs. Also, people from all social classes wore amulets, collars, and rings. Rich and poor alike believed that such items could protect them from harm. There was therefore always a great demand for all types of jewelry. Gold and gems, such as amethyst and turquoise, were widely available in Egypt. Silver and diamonds were not available, however, and had to be imported. The Egyptians made beads from a material called faience, composed mainly of quartz. This jewelry looked and felt like precious gems. Faience beads became very popular overseas and were an important export product.

Soft Metal, Strong Civilization

Iron was one important resource that ancient Egypt lacked. There was plenty of copper, but this was not as strong as iron. The metal industry lagged behind other industries in ancient Egypt. The Egyptians later learned how to make bronze, a much sturdier metal than copper, after they were attacked by the Hyksos in 1675 B.C. The Hyksos had used bronze weapons to fight the Egyptians. Even though Egypt lacked some metals, it did possess other important resources. The large amounts of gold, papyrus, and flax helped to make sure that the economy in ancient Egypt continued to grow, making Egypt one of the most powerful civilizations of ancient times.

Glossary

amulets (AM-yoo-lets) Something worn as a good luck charm.

craftsmen (KRAFTS-men) Workmen who practice a certain trade.

cultivated (KUL-tih-vayt-ed) Grown, as in, cultivated vegetables.

develop (dih-VEH-lup) Grow.

enamel (ih-NAH-mul) A paint used to make a smooth, hard surface.

export (ek-SPORT) Sending something to another place to be sold.

fertile (FER-tul) Good for making and growing things.

flax (FLAKS) A plant with blue flowers that is grown for its fiber.

fresco (FRES-koh) A painting done on wet plaster. Plaster is a mix of lime, sand, and water that hardens as it dries.

granite (GRA-nit) Melted rock that cooled and hardened beneath Earth's surface.

imported (im-PORT-ed) Brought from another country for sale or use.

industries (IN-dus-treez) Moneymaking businesses in which many people work and make money producing particular products.

limestone (LYM-stohn) A kind of rock.

materials (muh-TEER-ee-ulz) What things are made of.

pyramid (PEER-uh-mid) A large, stone structure with a square bottom and triangular sides that meet at a point on top.

quartz (KWORTZ) A very hard kind of rock.

resources (REE-sors-es) Things that occur in nature and that can be used or sold, such as gold, coal, or wool.

tombs (TOOMS) Graves.

Index

Primary Sources

Cover. Rekhmire inspects brickmaking and smelting workmen. Detail of a wall painting in the tomb of Rekhmire, vizier under Pharaohs Thutmose III and Amenophis II. Eighteenth Dynasty. **Inset.** Antelope vase. Pink limestone. Pre-Dynasty (circa 5000–3100 B.C.). **Page 4. Left.** Craftsmen building at a temple. Detail of a wall painting in the tomb of Rekhmire. Eighteenth Dynasty. **Right.** Fresco of fishing from the tomb of a sculptor named Ipy. 1279–1213 B.C. **Page 7. Top.** A scribe, Nebwani, leads an ox from Amarna tomb of Any. Eighteenth Dynasty. **Center.** Harvesting grain with sickles. Eighteenth Dynasty fresco. **Bottom.** Farmworkers making haystack. Bas-relief from tomb of Ti, official serving in reign of Kakai (2446–2426 B.C.) Fifth Dynasty. **Page 8.** Sculptors weighing gold and presenting their wares. Fresco from the tomb of sculptors Nebamon and Ipuky. Eighteenth Dynasty. **Right.** Wooden headrest. Fifth Dynasty. **Page 12. Top left.** Papyrus harvest, showing herdsmen, hunting, and dancing scenes. Painted relief from the tomb of Nefer and Kahay. Fifth Dynasty. **Right.** Furled papyrus and tools. Eighteenth Dynasty. **Page 15.** Vasemakers decorating a vase. Detail of a wall painting on the tomb of Rekhmire. Eighteenth Dynasty. **Inset.** Pottery vase. Pre-Dynasty. **Page 16. Top Left.** Two sculptors working on a statue. Painted limestone bas-relief. From the Mastaba of Kaemrehou. Fifth Dynasty. **Top Right.** Pharaoh Thutmose III. Black granite statue from Karnak. Eighteenth Dynasty. **Bottom.** Limestone pyramidion with relief of Sun God Re-Horakhty, as falcon and serpent Apep from Deir El Medina. Nineteenth Dynasty. **Page 19.** Model of a weaver's workshop. Eleventh Dynasty (2134–1991 B.C.). **Page 20. Top Left.** Gold and enamel uraeus snake belonging to the crown of King Sesostris II. From the pyramid of El Lahun. Twelfth Dynasty (circa 1880–1874 B.C.). **Center.** Funeral collar from the tomb of Pharaoh Tutankhamen. Eighteenth Dynasty. **Bottom.** Bracelet with motif of goddess Isis. Gold and cloisonne enamel. From the pyramid of Queen Amanishakheto. 1st century A.D.

Web Sites

Due to the changing nature of Internet links, PowerKids Press has developed an online list of Web sites related to the subject of this book. This site is updated regularly. Please use this link to access the list:

www.powerkidslinks.com/psaciv/econegy/